# Riot

by
**John Hall**
*Assistant Curate, St. Paul's Winchmore Hill, London*
*Formerly Senior Probation Officer, Tottenham*

GROVE BOOKS LIMITED
Bramcote    Nottingham    NG9 3DS

# CONTENTS

## THE COVER PICTURE

Is from a drawing by Dennis Bishop

'At the corner of Oxford Gardens, (Notting Hill, London), a lone cleric pleads for the trouble to stop. Beyond the police lines other squads seal off streets to avoid being outflanked.' (*The Independent* 2.9.1987).

*First Impression* December 1989

**ISSN** 0144-171X
**ISBN** 1 85174 132 1

# INTRODUCTION

Riots are nothing new to Britain. 'Easily led, easily persuaded, having nothing to lose, with generations of hardship, indifference and bitterness behind them . . . they became a mob. And thus spontaneously created a mob, they were urged to violence by that sensual, reactive impulse which brings a mob together and which forces it on to devastation, losing their identities in a fusing welter of destruction.' So wrote Christopher Hibbert, describing not the riots of the 1980s but the Gordon Riots of the 1780s.[1] Such outbreaks of violent disorder, though falling short of rebellion intended to topple the Government, have been and continue to be a disturbing feature of modern social life. Rioting is never far away, though many of us would wish that it were so.

We need to begin our journey accepting this fact, and then ask ourselves 'What can we do? What kind of response can we make?' The following pages offer a journey toward understanding, hope and healing? What kind of a social and historical event is called a 'riot'? Is a 'riot' simply an outbreak of pandemonium by youths with hearts set on evil intent—a 'riot' in the usual popular sense of the word, or is 'riot' better referred to as the legitimate expression of an oppressed people—in which case it might be called an 'uprising'? Whether 'riot' or 'uprising' is used, the popular language and definition of such events makes for powerful and pejorative statements being made which often go unchallenged and unexplored. I will be using the word 'riot', rather than 'uprising', 'public disorder', or 'hooliganism' simply because it is the most workable description, a view shared by other writers.[2] But if we are to make any headway we need first to listen carefully to the language being used, which attributes very different, even contradictory meanings to the violent events taking place.

It has been said that, 'After a great riot there is much to be cleared away: the rubble, the burned out cars, the broken glass. But then, for weeks afterwards, there is work to do clearing away the thick layer of nonsense which sifts down like ash from the stratosphere upon us all.'[3] So we need to ask ourselves what sense we can make of these events. Are there any signposts in this complex and controversial business? Lord Scarman's Report after the Brixton Disorders of 1981 offers some useful pointers gleaned from the ashes of bitter experience.[4] Social Science may also guide us toward an explanation of such behaviour, though it has yet to establish for us 'the cause' of riot. Such signposts as there are, both in official reports and in Social Science, fall short of providing a fully adequate explanation of riot behaviour. This is not entirely a bad thing, for in recognizing that no one secular explanation has all the answers, there remains the need for and indeed scope for fresh creative thinking, not least by Christians, who in my experience have found such events as difficult as anyone to come to terms with.

[1] C. Hibbert *King Mob* (Longmans, Green 1958) p.92.
[2] M. LeRoy *Riots in Liverpool 8: Some Christian Responses* (ECUM 1984) p.3.
[3] N. Ascherson in *Sunday Observer* 13.10.85
[4] Lord Scarman *The Scarman Report* (reprint Pelican 1986).

Alongside the search for an explanation of riot events, it seems important to identify and examine the key social issues which are repeatedly associated with riots. Relative deprivation, if not outright oppression, is a key element. Racism, unemployment, poor policing, poverty, and powerlessness march alongside. Christians in riot areas have much to say on these points, and some of the most useful material in this booklet arose out of a survey of clergy views undertaken in the summer of 1987.

But how is the Christian, who believes in a loving God, to understand these events and the social evils which accompany them? What are the varieties of response which are legitimate options for Christians? On the one extreme, it is fair to ask, 'should Christians ever riot?', and on the other, 'Is non-violence always appropriate?'. Christians need to know what the parameters are within which to frame their own response to riots, whether to be non-violent or to be violent, and what to do and what not to do. In order to address these and other questions our attention is forcefully turned to our theology. We will therefore need to look at what kind of theology can and needs to be done.

So where can one turn, where has the thinking been done? Personally, I have not been able to find a single Christian book tackling the subject of riot. That is not to say there is no useful resource material to turn to, there clearly is. For example, The World Council of Churches has struggled with the issue of 'non-violence' as it has discussed how to respond to Apartheid in South Africa. But the paucity of Christian material relating directly to riots on mainland Britain led me to undertake some research of my own.

An exploratory survey I undertook in 1987 involved Anglican clergy working in areas of Britain which had seen riots in the 1980s (namely Birmingham, Brixton, Bristol, Liverpool, and Tottenham). The respondents identified the dominant theological issue as concerning the Christian's identification with the poor and oppressed. There were other important issues raised too, for example, justice and peace. The clergy as resident professionals make a particular contribution to our understanding of riot.

My objective is to reach a point of Biblical and social awareness which will provide a Christian rationale for an ethically appropriate response to riot. I ought to say at the outset that I cannot see any justification for Christians in today's Britain to riot. This does not mean I place myself with those who see Romans 13.1-7 as laying a mandatory duty upon Christians always to submit to the authorities. Such a view would be an erroneous interpretation of this text.[1] But it is hard to imagine when it might be necessary to riot in Britain in order to defend an oppressed individual or people. (Some people may consider the situation in Northern Ireland to be an exception). Taking the Broadwater Farm riot in 1985 as a case in point, I found this riot lacking a justifiable motive at the outset and resulting in nothing other than tragedy at its end. This is the standard pattern. By and large riot is a

---

[1] See *The Kairos Document—A Theological Comment on The Political Crisis in S. Africa* (Eerdmans 1986) Ch. 2

social evil. Riots leave victims. People die; many are injured; and property and livelihoods are destroyed. The effects stay with individuals and communities for many years. We are all its victims, as it is a part of our corporate life.

But riot does not occur in splendid isolation from other social evils. Indeed people often find the burden and consequences of these other evils to be so great, it would be very suprising if violence did not almost naturally occur. First impressions of riots and rioters are usually far from the whole truth. Although almost always it is the question of order and law which steals the national media headlines, the oppression and deprivation of individuals and communities lying behind a riot barely get attention at all.

Consequently whenever a riot occurs it proves difficult, especially in the immediate aftermath to get behind the pejorative language, emotive criticism, and judgmental attitudes to ask the important questions—'Why did this riot happen?' and 'What ought to be done now?' In my experience many people, both those from within the community which has directly experienced the riot and those who live outside, get stuck at the point of making moral judgments. Sadly, some never move beyond it. No one is listening to anyone else! A golden rule when looking at riot seems to me to be—listen to what people are saying and refrain from passing swift judgment. Jesus himself took this approach to the woman caught in the act of adultery.[1]

This leads us into the final section of the booklet which addresses the practical question, 'What response should we, as Christians make to riot events?' A variety of approaches which can be made, before—during—and after the riot are outlined in what follows. The Handsworth and Aston Churches' 'Crisis Procedure' is a helpful model, and involves specified Christians being on the streets.[2]

Finally I wish to record my debt of gratitude for the 'stories' of clergy and laity; for the 'stories' of young people who have for one reason or another been caught up in the riot and the aftermath; for the examples of understanding and professional 'care' of my former colleagues in the Probation Service; and for the shared lives of those people most closely affected by the riots, whose wealth of experience has fed my life so much and has contributed toward my trying to ensure that all can find here some response appropriate to their situation however near or far removed riot seems to be.

[1] See John 8.3ff.
[2] *The Crisis Procedure*—Available from: The Legal Advice Service, United Evangelical Project, 29 Trinity Road, Aston, Birmingham, B6.

# 1. RIOTS AND HISTORY

Let us begin by looking at the place of riot in Britain. 'Rioting is at least as English as thatched cottages and honey still for tea,'[1] reported one newspaper after the 1985 Tottenham riots. There is some truth here for the civil unrest in our towns and cities in the 1980s is not without historical precedent. Historically, there have been many riots in Britain, and the tradition of rioting has seen its most serious expression in our urban centres.

The Gordon Riots of 1780 are perhaps best known. The severity of this particular conflict in London led to the deaths of not less than 850 people. Not suprisingly, these riots caused considerable alarm and consternation. As the historian Trevelyan wrote, 'With no police, save watchmen whose proceedings were a constant theme of mockery, with criminal laws that by their careless ferocity and irregular execution fostered crime, the mob of that period was a fearful thing. In the riots of 1780 it went near to burning down London.'[2] Christopher Hibbert's *King Mob*[3], vividly describes those events, and, to my mind, the contemporary parallels, in terms of both the course of the riot and the social issues raised, are inescapable.

In London, the founding of Peel's 'new police' accompanied much-needed law reforms in the nineteenth century and therefore prevented any further serious clash between the armed forces and the working classes. Trevelyan's assessment is that, 'had there been "Peelers" in Manchester in 1819, or in Bristol in 1831, there would have been no Peterloo, and no burning of Bristol . . . There had previously been no force capable of doing anything with a London mob short of shooting or sabring.'[4] The role of the 'Peelers'' modern counterpart, the police, inevitably attracts much controversy, as they seek to keep the peace.

The clergy at the time of the Gordon Riots (1780); the Luddite Riots (1812); Peterloo (1819); and the Bristol Riots (1831); were closely allied with the Government and the authorities. At the local level, the clergy were closely identifed with both the squirearchy and the magistracy. Indeed the violent partisanship of the clergy against the New Radicalism brought them into popular odium in the days of Peterloo. It was only the Methodists who, in the view of Trevelyan, had a thought to spare for that 'mass of beings, physically and morally corrupt' who were to be found in every town and city.'[5] This raises for us in sharp relief the question of the church's role in society and more especially at times of such civil disorder. More recently the church has arguably sought to adopt a more appropriate response, voicing and championing the concerns of the poor and oppressed. The *Faith In The City* report of The Archbishop of Canterbury's Commission being the best known example.[6] Christians can never adopt the position of mere observers of the social scene, the Parable of the Good Samaritan reminds us of that. (Luke 6.10f.) If there is a lesson for Christians from the past it is that we need to begin by repenting of our own past failings.

[1] N. Ascherson in *Sunday Observer* 13 October 1985.
[2] G. Trevelyan *British History in the 19th cent. and after: 1782-1919* (Pelican 1965) p.20.
[3] C. Hibbert *King Mob* (Longmans Green 1958).
[4] *Ibid.* p.203.
[5] *Ibid.* pp.39-40.
[6] ACUPA Report *Faith In The City* (CHP 1985).

In the twentieth century there were serious riots in Britain in 1919 after the First World War. All the larger sea ports were the scenes for 'race riots' against Britain's 'black' seamen. Riots also occurred elsewhere. In Luton troops were called when rioters razed the Town Hall. In Liverpool rioters were dealt with by bayonet-wielding troops and the deployment of tanks, and in London, throughout the summer of 1919 youths fought with police in familiar-sounding places—Brixton, Tottenham and Wood Green.

In the 1930s (a period often compared with today because of its high unemployment), there were such serious disturbances as to earn it the tag, 'the devil's decade'. However, in popular thinking this period is often recalled today through rose-tinted spectacles as a period of peace and tranquillity. Mrs. Thatcher herself is quoted as saying on a number of occasions, 'we had much higher unemployment in the 1930s, but we didn't get violence then.'[1] This was patently not the case.

In October 1931, for example, violence was much in evidence as the following account shows: 'mounted police charged the unemployed in Salford; more rioting in Glasgow; 80,000 unemployed march in Manchester: police turn hoses on them; ...violent clashes between police and unemployed in London, Blackburn and Cardiff.'[2] The fact is this century has repeatedly seen rioting as a feature of contemporary life.

The pattern of riots continued to the present decade, when a new wave of riots began with the St. Paul's riots in Bristol. The following year, 1981, saw widespread rioting throughout Britain, of a ferocity and significance beyond anything seen for many years outside of Northern Ireland. (Brixton, Toxteth, Southall, and Mosside will be familiar names).

In the period since then the riots of 1982 and 1985 were the most serious, this time Handsworth (Lozells), Toxteth, Brixton and Tottenham were the main locations. Such was the political impact of these events that, following the General Election in 1987, the 'reclaiming of the Inner Cities' featured as the main headline in the Queen's Speech.[3] It is the riots which have drawn attention to the divisions in society and have placed the social issues associated with the rioters' communities on the current political agenda. Yet it would be over-optimistic to assume that, whatever political initiatives may emerge, riots will cease to be a feature of modern social life. There are now reports in the press of riots in provincial towns, and *The Independent* headline reads, 'Rural Rioters Confront Police'.[4]

This historical overview shows that riots have been and continue to be a feature of social life, and possibly more so than one might at first imagine. It is also readily apparent that the issues riots raise are both complex and controversial. Riots, whenever and wherever they occur, raise a wide range of, political, economic, social and religious questions. The first question then to beg an answer is, 'What sense can be made of riots?'

[1] Quoted in J. Benyon *A Tale of Failure: Race and Policing* (ESRC University of Warwick 1986) p.101. Appendix B contains a detailed analysis of riots in the 1930s.
[2] *Ibid.* p.101.
[3] *The Independent* 26 June 1987 front page.
[4] *The Independent* 10 June 1988 p.3.

## 2. CAN WE MAKE SENSE OF RIOTS?

As Halsbury's *Laws of England* defines it,
'Riot is a tumultuous disturbance of the peace by three or more per-
sons assembled together with an intent mutually to assist one another
by force, if necessary, against anyone who opposes them in the
execution of their common purpose, and who execute or begin to
execute that common purpose in a violent manner so as to alarm at
least one person of reasonable firmness and courage.'[1]

Riots in Britain in the 1980s compare in terms of their ferocity neither
with the riots of earlier days nor with urban riots abroad.[2] (In Detroit in
1967, for example, 30 people were killed in just one night of rioting).

It is what these recent riot events 'say' about the contemporary society,
which is their context, that seems so fundamentally important to hear.
William Cobbett wrote of the Luddite riots of 1812, 'Measures ought to
be adopted, not so much for putting an end to riots, as to prevent the misery out of which they arise.'[3] Lord Scarman, in his report on *The Brixton
Disorders 10-12 April 1981*[4] was likewise concerned in his causal
analysis to separate and make explicit the precipitating factors which led
to the actuality of the riot and the underlying long-term factors which set
up a potential for riot. The riots of history echo each other in their clamour
to be understood. (It is beyond the scope of this booklet to look at either
the particular issues of Northern Ireland or riots arising out of Football
Hooliganism).

Ought one then to see violent dissent as the hallmark of a divided society
in danger of disintegration, or as the welcome harbinger of much-needed
reform? In what sense are riots as Martin Luther King put it, 'The voice of
the unheard'? There is a most important truth here, which lays upon us a
fundamental duty to hear and understand what kind of an event has been
taking place and to refrain from passing too swift a judgment on it and its
participants.

### Competing Voices
The central problem is to decide which of the competing voices to believe.
Should the rioters themselves offer the best explanation as to their
motives and behaviour, or do the police on the spot provide the best
understanding? Maybe the judiciary, the magistrates and judges, can best
weigh up the evidence and provide a clear explanation of what took place
and why? What about the media for an unbiased report? Perhaps the civic
and religious leaders can offer an explanation? Or how about approaching
a few academic sociologists? All these people have their own perspective,
if not bias, and there is in my opinion no one place where an 'objective'
account can be found. There is no way round taking responsibility oneself
to listen, to pray, to reflect, and to act.

[1] Scarman *ibid.* p.73
[2] See for example O. Kerner *Report of the National Advisory Commission on Civil Disorders*
(Bantam Books N.Y. 1968) on the U.S. civil rights riots of the 1960s.
[3] From Cobbett's newspaper the *Political Register*, reported in J. Marlow's *The Peterloo
Massacre* (Panther 1969) p.34.
[4] Scarman *ibid* (reprint)

## Scarman's wisdom

Lord Scarman's report produced after the Brixton Riots of 1981 is a good place to start, listening as he does to the many different voices clamouring for our attention and approval. Although Lord Scarman produced his report at the request of the Government, and it may be thought to be less than radical because of it, the undoubted integrity of Lord Scarman himself and the status of this 'official' report have given it widespread respect.

Scarman identified various long-term factors which he saw as giving rise to a potential for riot in Brixton. These were:
(1) Demographic. The community contained a disproportionate number of deprived and vulnerable people. (Scarman 2.13)
(2) An inner city area in an advanced state of social and economic decay. (Scarman 2.1—2.11)
(3) Racial discrimination. 'The ethnic minority groups suffer the same deprivations. . . but much more acutely.' (Scarman 2.35)
(4) A high crime rate where police/community relations were at a low ebb. (Scarman 4.1—4.46)
(5) The feeling of political insecurity and lack of representation of black and the ethnic minority communities. (Scarman 2.36)

Given the seriousness of these underlying problems in Brixton, it took only a minor event to trigger the potential into an actual riot. The massive police presence in 'Operation Swamp' was in Scarman's view that triggering event. Scarman also identified three other causes:
(1) 'Fun value'. (Scarman 3.109)
(2) 'Looting', which drew in outsiders. (Scarman 3.61)
(3) 'Media coverage'. It also drew in outsiders. (Scarman 3.92).

On the basis of this explanation Scarman made his recommendations:
(1) The inner cities' problems needed a co-ordinated approach. (Scarman 8.44)
(2) In the areas of housing, education and employment, policies are needed to combat the racial discrimination and disadvantage which the ethnic minorities experience. (Scarman 8.45—8.52)
(3) Police reforms are needed, including how to police riots. (Scarman 8.13—42)
(4) Law reform is needed, particularly in the area relating to powers of arrest, police complaint procedure, and political demonstration.

Some attempt to implement these reforms has been made following the publication of Lord Scarman's report, though not without much controversy. Notwithstanding the Scarman report's worthy contribution to our understanding of the Brixton riots, the report should be seen neither as the ultimate authority on riot, nor as the sole herald of utopian social reforms necessary to keep the peace. Scarman is a salutory reminder that nothing
'exempts us from attempting to discern the factors , some of them having emerged particularly in the last few years, which have contributed to what Lord Scarman referred to as "the complex pattern of conditions which lies at the root of the disorders in Brixton and elsewhere".'[1]

[1] *Faith In The City* para. 8.48.

## Gifford's wisdom

The Gifford Report[1], on the Broadwater Farm disturbances in Tottenham in 1985 is one example of a more critical and recent study. Arguably, Gifford exposes more clearly than Scarman the underlying and persisting tensions present in a community. The report gives central place to the people and community life of the Broadwater Farm Estate, and looks at the 'disturbances' in this context. The fact that the Broadwater Farm Inquiry was initiated by the Labour controlled Haringey Council, which itself had fought long and hard political battles with the Conservative Government of Mrs. Thatcher, also give it a more independent and radical perspective. The Gifford Report is outspoken in its criticism of the police approach to riot, one of 'being armed as if to put down an enemy.' Rather the Report urges that problems in a community be faced by 'getting around the table in an amicable way with the community.' Central Government is roundly criticized for failing to address the problems of those living on the estate.

His second report produced at the end of 1988 after the trials at the Central Criminal Court were finally over, was critical of both the police handling of the prosecutions and the London Borough of Haringey's unwillingness to consult with the police. It also pointed out the continuing problems of the Broadwater Farm Estate where for example the unemployment rate is four times the national average.

## Social Science and Riot

Stan Taylor, a sociologist at the University of Warwick, has looked at the Scarman analysis against a wide range of theoretical and political perspectives on corporate violence. Taylor's analysis provides a very useful framework in the search for sense behind riot events.[2]

Taylor says there are two main groups of theories which stress the importance of social relations, social institutions and social systems as causes of riot. One group of theories look at society as if it were essentially and naturally in a state of continuing conflict, and outbreaks of riotous behaviour are the norm. A second group of theories take the opposite approach and see society as if it were essentially harmonious and where there is a natural consensus to be found. In this case riots are an aberration from the norm.

### . . . (1) Society as essentially in a state of conflictF:

Among the sociological theories of riot which see society as essentially in conflict, the class struggles of Marxism are familiar ground, riots being examples of the proletariat rising up against the capitalist 'bosses'. Some Marxists go as far as seeing 'race' itself as a 'class', and 'race riots' as instances of protest by the exploited races about to see in a racial revolution. Other sociologists see society as comprised of groups with competing interests arising from different life-chances. The latter theorists explain riots 'as the protests of consistent losers anxious to achieve some redistribution of resources in their favour.'[3] Aspects of such an analysis carry conviction, are reflected even in an official report such as Scarman's, and should be seriously evaluated (even if you find a section like this difficult to read and harder going!).

[1] *The Broadwater Farm Inquiry* Lord Gifford ISBN 0 9511604 0 0.
[2] In J. Benyon *Scarman and After* (Pergamon 1984).
[3] *Ibid* p.22.

## . . . (2) Society as essentially in a state of harmony:

The alternative sociological approach gives emphasis to the moral cohesiveness of a consensus society where the social order is maintained through the exercise of social controls. A process of socialization takes place, fitting people into an accepted social order. This portrays a society which can successfully bring up all its citizens to behave 'properly'.

The consensus theorists argue that it is when the social system fails to operate and respond adequately that riots occur, like a hiccup in the normally smooth flow of social life. Smelser, using this model, argued that a temporary system failure gives rise to a 'potential' for collective violence, the 'actual' violence only arising after some precipitating event.[1] Many theorists adopted this approach to explain the 1960s race riots in the U.S. For the most part they found, for example, that the lack of openness of municipal institutions to black demands was positively correlated with rioting. (Racism is often wrongly considered as simply operating at the personal level. In fact racism operates at an institutional level too). The research into the rioting of the 1960s in the U.S.showed that rioting was more likely to be avoided where reform was considered. Notice here the similarities between the consensus model and the Scarman analysis!

## Conflict or consensus?

Both conflict and consensus sociological theories seem to me to have identified important foundational issues in trying to understand riot. Any adequate theoretical understanding of riot needs to address and embrace these twin approaches to society.

## Riot from tension and frustration:

There are a number of theories of a socio-psychological nature which seek to explain collective violence. These explain riots as individual behaviours determined by particular psychological processes. Festinger's theory of 'cognitive dissonance' has been used as the basis for an explanation of riots by a number of people.[2] All that this means is that when people don't get what they are led to expect from life, they show it! If then, for example, unemployment rises in an area to an unbearable level and the normal political channels fail to remedy the tension it creates, then riot may quite naturally follow. The growth of and pressure from the media and the consumer society today have greatly increased pressures of this kind.

Besides the 'cognitive dissonance' approach, there are also theories which focus on the 'frustration/aggression' model of behaviour.[3] The argument here is that people whose goals are blocked then become frustrated. This frustration if sustained then becomes changed into aggression and violence. The pent-up feelings of frustration at the deprivation, past, present, or anticipated, become as it were 'exorcized' through riot.

It is worth noting that both groups of theories use explanations of riotous behaviour which contain the notion of the individual's non- rationality, the rioter responding violently to unconscious or uncontrollable inner mental processes. Such an understanding has its place, but may pay insufficient regard to the human 'will', our ability to be decision-makers.

[1] N.Smelser *Theory of collective behaviour* (Routledge 1962).
[2] L. Festinger *The Theory of Cognitive Dissonance* (Stanford 1978).
[3] J. Dollard et al *Frustration and Aggression* (Yale 1974).

## Riot for economic gain:

Economic theories of riot are quite different in that they emphasize not the irrationality of behaviour, but its rationality—riot as a chosen course of action based upon economic considerations. Gain (through looting), loss (through apprehension by the police), gain (through the entertainment value), and loss (through the penalties imposed by the court) can all be seen as entering into the economic equation.

This economic approach seems plausible and could be developed further. Indeed little research has been done in this area. Support for such an approach can probably be found in Scarman, who identified a group of rioters who primarily went to the riot for the looting, some even travelling from outside the immediate area to do so. There were those too whom Scarman saw who rioted for the excitement value, for the thrill of the occasion where high risks could perhaps be traded for high status and satisfaction in an otherwise monochrome and routine pattern of life. Personally I am convinced that the rioter's belief that something might be gained, whether material or status, helps explain riot.

## Riot—An aspect of Politics?:

Political variables have been stressed in various theories as holding the key to understanding riots. One group argues that extreme political groups engineer riots in order for example to destabilize society. The media—TV, radio, and popular press—have given most support to the idea that such groups as drug barons, or Trotskyists, or National Front sympathizers master-minded the riot. These ideas can lead to over-reaction by the authorities, even if they are by and large swiftly discredited subsequently. Suggestions of this kind were made concerning the Broadwater Farm riot, allegations which were to my knowledge without any foundation. Such allegations give power to the elbow of the authorities who may wish to impose strict controls on an area after a riot. On the Broadwater Farm estate saturation policing followed the disturbances, and the identification of a scapegoat enables such measures to be more easily justified. Scapegoats can also be used to justify decisions not to fund remedial projects in an area for fear they might fall into the scapegoat's hands.

Another group argues that the institutions take time to respond to changes in society and riot occupies 'the gap' between the period of a change and the necessary adaptation to bring it effectively within the control of the social system. For example, unemployment created by macro-economic forces depresses an area, and it is only many months if not years later that political remedies take positive effect.

Another theory is a variant on the last, but sees the taking of time to make adaptive changes as a matter of deliberate choice by the social institutions. Bachrach and Baratz argue from this viewpoint, suggesting that, 'political elites may mobilize bias to make non-decisions, decisions not to let particular demands become part of the political process. For any group thus excluded, riots offer a way of forcing demands into the political system, of accomplishing through violence what they see themselves unable to achieve by more conventional means.'[1] Again, reading Scarman, one sees that the black population felt excluded from and rejected by

[1] From S. Taylor in J. Benyon *Scarman and After* page 25.

the normal political processes. Feelings of political impotence and rejection have long been recognized as generating public disorder. Whether the state has intentionally created these feelings or not, the sad truth has to be faced, that such political deprivations do exist in Britain today.

A final variant on theories based around political variables is one that argues that riots are a response to coercive political repression. It has been shown that there is a positive correlation between increased state coercion and the outbreak of riotous behaviour. Scarman identified the police 'Operation Swamp' as the event which triggered the Brixton riot. The police in such circumstances have to walk a tightrope between maintaining the peace without precipitating a riot. Sometimes they fail. David Sheppard and Derek Warlock's observations on the streets of Toxteth as recorded in *Better Together*[1] describe how policing can be perceived as hostile action.

## Riot—Copy-cat and other causes:
Social science also has a cluster of theories which suggest that one riot can start another. The 'contagious' factors in riot (ie. geography, the media coverage, and a riot tradition in an area), have all been put forward as causes of riot. What happens in South Africa can, for example, precipitate disturbances elsewhere. Scarman again lends some measure of support here. Sheppard and Worlock describe how large numbers of outsiders drawn into an area of unrest can spark off further disturbances.

## The views of the politicians:
Taylor has usefully identified the explanation of riots offered by three dominant political views. Each brings its own interpretation and meaning to such events. These Taylor calls the conservative, liberal and radical views. There are of course other shades of political opinion.

*(1) The conservative view* sees existing democratic instituitions as adequate to meet the needs of deprived groups, and the ballot-box obviates the need for any collective violence. Individuals who riot are seen as examples of 'manipulated, morally degenerate and irrational mass behaviour: riots are to be avoided by effective policing, moral regeneration, and the exercise of responsibility by the media.'[2]

A conservative criticism of Scarman would argue that, given the availability of democratic machinery, the role of deprivation as a cause of riot was overstressed at the expense of other factors. Other riots did not always occur in such deprived areas and where there was such a marked ethnic minority presence. Police repression would be seen as over-emphasized by Scarman, for after all, as Scarman noted riots stil occured in the West Midlands in 1981 where police-community relations were more favourable. The riots were, the conservative might argue, the product of immoral and irrational behaviour by degenerate youths. The solution therefore would not be economic and social reforms, but moral regeneration through inculcating respect for parents, police and the authorities.

[1] D. Sheppard and D. Worlock, *Better Together* (Hodder and Stoughton 1987) ch.6
[2] From S. Taylor in J. Benyon *Scarman and After* p.26.

*(2) The liberal view* of riot behaviour is that sometimes the deprived groups can become unrepresented in society. The liberal answer therefore to the collective violence which emerges, lies in the making of reforms and redistributing power and resources downwards towards the poor and oppressed.

A liberal criticism of Scarman would criticize any deviation of stress in the report away from riots as the product of economic, social and political deprivation. The 'conspiracy' theory, and the 'fun and profit' motives for riot mentioned in Scarman would be seen as diverting attention away from the real need for the policy makers to make the necesary reforms and redistribution of power and resources.

*(3) The radical view* argues from a perspective which sees society as having a dominant class or other groups who seek to maintain through the social structures their position. State control through increased coercion, reforms, or concessions do nothing to deal with the fundamental inequalities. 'Only successful revolution can create a society from which violence will vanish.'[1]

A radical criticism of Scarman would centre on the fact that a radical perspective was not included in the report. There was for example, on the one hand, no Marxist analysis of the macro-structures of society and consequently no recommendation for the wholesale reform of the riot-causing capitalist structures, and on the other hand, no Marxist call for revolution.

Making sense of riots is then a complex and controversial business, and each of the three views outlined above is inadequate on its own. Our present understanding of the subject does not provide any one hard-and-fast theory, but it does provide useful theoretical signposts and alerts one to the kind of political perspectives at work. Much more work needs to be done before we can understand the nature and causes of social violence. In the meantime one needs to use the available theoretical material critically.

What is particularly interesting to me is that there appears to be an underlying continuity of meaning to the riots of recent years. The same threads keep reappearing in the tapestry. There is, I believe, an emerging picture, with a meaning to be grasped. Riot is not the result of individual delinquency, but a product of the society we live in. There is also an historical continuity in the picture of riot. As Pearson puts it, 'The forms, categories and images which are brought to bear in the modern social thought and practice which fixes its gaze on "deviance" were born out of the confrontation with the dangerous energies of King Mob' (in 1780).[2] Beside continuity of meaning and history, there is also discontinuity too. There are new aspects of riot to consider—for example, the modern media; the movement of the middle class professionals to homes outside the area; and, modern policing methods which incidentally mean putting mainly white policemen into non-white areas.

[1] Benyon *ibid.* p.27.
[2] G Pearson *The Deviant Imagination* (Macmillan 1975) p.145.

# 3. RIOTS AND SOCIAL ISSUES

What are the key social issues which are repeatedly associated with riots? The inner city and urban priority areas of Britain reflected such 'acute human misery' that the Archbishop of Canterbury set up his Commission on Urban Priority areas in 1983. The resultant ACUPA report, *Faith In The City* was published two years later after the autumn riots of 1985. Part One of the report goes some way to describe the recent history of British cities—'one of economic, physical and social decay.'[1] Like the Scarman report before it, which pointed to the 'failure of many attempts over the last three decades to tackle the problem of inner city decline', reference to the social problems urban people faced could not be avoided.

Since the 1977 Government White Paper, *Policy for the Inner Cities*[2], the central government has also recognized the serious situation in the cities, though there is still in 'conservative politics' a reluctance to attribute a cause of riots to social deprivation. There has also been a significant contradiction in government thinking between approaches to tackle the problems of the city and the steps thought to be necessary to deal with public order and riots. Various measures have been taken on two fronts to try and improve the situation, but these have sometimes acted against each other. (For example, increased police presence to combat the social problem of increased crime in an area has had the adverse effect of triggering a riot). There are no easy answers in trying to keep public order whilst protecting civil liberties.

Scarman wrote, 'While good policing can help diminish tension and avoid disorder, it cannot remove the causes of social stress where these are to be found, as those in Brixton and elsewhere are, deeply embedded in fundamental economic and social conditions. Any attempt to resolve the circumstances from which the disorders ... sprang cannot therefore be limited to recommendations about policing but must embrace the wider context.'[3] What then are the causes of social stress which lead to young male adults and children rioting?

## Common Factors:

What are the tension-creating social issues of the inner city? Colin Bedford has provided a typical list of 'Common Factors' which add to tension in the cities.[4] He identifies from his experience as a clergyman in Toxteth, Liverpool:
- unemployment and lack of job opportunities
- growing numbers of educated unemployable
- adaptation of technology, automation and the microchip making an increasingly soulless working environment
- inadequate housing, and often poor associated public amenities
- political infighting, and changing policies causing public frustration
- lack of confidence in public servants, who themselves seem overwhelmed by the size of the tasks they have been commissioned to do

[1] ACUPA *Faith in the City* (CHP 1985) p.3.
[2] *Policy For The Inner Cities* (White Paper HMSO 1977).
[3] Scarman *ibid.* section 6.1.
[4] C. Bedford *Weep for the City* (Lion 1982) pp.13-14.

- increase in violence, petty crime, mugging, burglaries
- racial tension, through minorities suffering serious deprivation
- police-community relations at a low ebb, under-staffed forces cannot cope with the job that society demands of them
- current financial recession causing further frustration as other demands on government spending take priority
- a feeling of powerlessness as most of those 'in power'—in finance, government, trade unions, management—do not live in the major cities nor do they understand those who do
- major shifts in work centres from the inner city to industrial estates and suburbs, making transport costs higher for those in work
- increasing number of broken homes, one-parent families and insecure children

Not all these features listed by Colin Bedford will be present in any one place or at any one time, but they are very familiar ground to those with experience of such areas. The list is also incomplete as we shall see.

**Riot specific factors : Views from the Clergy:**
In order to tie down more precisely the social issues associated with riots and not just the problems of the inner cities, (though the two proved to be closely correlated), I undertook a survey of clergy views in the summer of 1987. All the clergy approached were in areas where riots had taken place. I first asked them the question, 'What do you think are the main social issues raised by recent civil disturbance in our inner cities?' Eleven out of nineteen clergy replied.

The question was deliberately phrased to avoid asking for 'causes' of riot. I wanted to elicit a response that would throw up a cluster of social issues associated in the respondent's mind with riot, to cast the net as broadly as possible. I was not trying to prove what the causes of riot were, that was beyond the exercise. It is the task for the social scientist to demonstrate significant links between social criteria and riot, and to date what research I have seen has yet to 'prove' that unemployment, for example, causes riot. What the available literature does suggest is that each riot needs to be looked at separately and that a wide variety of social issues are involved. Having said this, it is nonetheless very revealing to identify what the social issues associated with riot are from the results of my own survey.

**(1) The main issues—'Racism', 'Unemployment' and 'Policing':**
An analysis of the replies I received indicates a close but not unexpected parallel with the common factors of inner city life listed by Colin Bedford above. My own survey had the advantage of giving some measure of relative importance to individual riot-linked criteria, and the replies show that two social issues, namely 'racism' and 'unemployment', closely followed by a third, 'policing' were held to be the most important. (Eight of the eleven respondents specifically identified racism as a social issue raised by the recent disturbances. An equal number mentioned unemployment, and seven of eleven identified policing together with factors such as crime, justice, and law and order.) Racism is behaviour based on prejudices about ethnic minorities and black people. The resultant racial discrimination results in a lack of equal opportunity, and prevents fair

access to a whole range of social 'goods' which the 'white' community take for granted. Racism is unjust and intolerable, and operates at both the personal and institutional levels.

The three different factors often worked together in the replies, for example, the combined effect of racism with unemployment was noted. Another example where two issues worked together is 'racist policing'. Though mentioned most often, the three issues of racism, unemployment and policing do not stand in isolation from the other social issues.

**(2) The other issues—'Powerlessness', 'Politics', and 'Poverty':**
Close on the heals of the big issues and often associated with them was 'powerlessness', often expressed in terms of disatisfaction with politics. Many inner city people do not feel they have a political voice. 'Poverty' was specifically mentioned as an issue by five respondents, though if one broadened out the definition of 'poverty' to include the poverty of housing, education and welfare services, then 'poverty' should be included in with the big three above.

What may appear surprising is that so few respondents saw family life stress as an issue. Suprising, because some leading politicians, would have us believe that the root of these social issues lies within the family and not within the wider social structures.

What is clear from this survey, is that riot has relatively little association with stresses within family life (though stresses there often are), but rather more association with other issues, racism and unemployment heading the list by a short head. Further, this survey strengthens the view that any serious attempt to look at riot events has to face the social issues which emerge. It would, of course,be unwise to push the results of this survey too far, for one reason it represents the views of a single group, the local clergy. However, my own experience of working in the Probation Service in areas where serious rioting occurred would make my own answers to the survey very similar to those of the clergy.

**What about 'alienation'?:**
On the basis of my own contact with offenders, their families, and their friends, perhaps I would have given greater emphasis to the degree of alienation felt and experienced by those who riot. This is an alienation from what other sections of British society accept as normal—a rising standard of living, employment, freedom from discrimination, a home, and social and political power. The *Faith in the City* Report rather boldly identified alienation as a cause of disorder, and 'it is difficult to exaggerate how alienated these young people are. [And] this alienation is closely related to unemployment.' It continues, 'Alienation—the making of people, not least young people, to feel themselves to be "outsiders" is from a particular border that is felt to be unresponsive and uncaring'.[1]

Particularly alienating is unemployment, and the lack of work for school leavers is tantamount to denying these young people adulthood. Within the Probation Service I was aware that the criminal careers of young offenders in the Tottenham area were being extended beyond the teens and even into the late twenties, mainly it seemed, because of long-term unemployment. It should come as little suprise that such alienated young people riot.

[1] *Faith in the City ibid.* paras. 13.95-98.

# 4. HOPE AND HEALING

**First—the story:**
We need to start by 'listening'. First by listening to history, and then to the competing voices which help us to make sense of riot events, for there is neither a 'theology of riot' nor 'a portion of scripture' which can be read off as *the* word on riots. My first objective has been therefore to 'tell the story' of riot, of what it is, and what the 'common factors' associated with riot are.

The fact that Christians have often failed to listen goes some way to explain how Christians come to understand and respond to riot events so very differently. Webber, for example, found that some churches separated themselves from the riot events and kept their heads down. Others linked their church closely with the interests of the State was expressed by government. Still others, as 'salt and light' in the world sought to engage with the riot events which took place.[1]

The danger in starting with theology is that we can simply use it to justify our own presuppositions. It is as we expose theology and the Bible to the social issues of our time such as riot and allow the two to interact in a process of critical reflection that an adequate and dynamic theology is formed. I like to think of this as 'doing theology'.

In the Genesis story of creation the Bible tells us that God intended mankind to live in harmonious relationships with him and with fellow humans. Through the Fall these relations became spoiled, and consequently, where human is pitted against human, as in a riot, we see relations which are less than the loving ideal God intended. Jesus Christ came to make good the human condition, and he called all people to join him in this task. He preached the Kingdom of God, a place where people were to love God and love their neighbour as themselves—a Kingdom known now and in the age to come. Jesus gave Christians the Holy Spirit to continue his work on earth offering a way of hope and healing. Christians are called to enter into Christ's work in his world.

**Second—Reflecting on 'the story':**
In my own survey, the clergy in riot areas of Britain were asked the question, 'What do you think are the main theological issues raised by the recent civil disturbance in our cities?' One vicar in Tottenham wrote, 'Many people I speak to, especially young black people, see the church as part of the system which oppresses them.' His was a typical reply. Responding to this, this clergyman was one of many to emphasize the importance of the Christian's identification with the poor and oppressed. A concern for justice was also given much support. To their mind such popular views as, 'this is a "Christian country"' (with its over-identification of church with State), and 'matters of faith are to be seen as essentially private and individualistic' (with its unbiblical separation of private and public life)

[1] *The Secular Saint* (Zonervan 1979) 1979

were given no support whatsoever. Rather they came up with a radical Christian approach along the following lines:

## (1) Identifying with the poor and oppressed:

Various clergy referred to *The Kairos Document—A Theological comment on the Political Crisis in South Africa*[1] and the publications of 'The Urban Training Unit' in Sheffield as sources of relevant theology. 'We need our own liberation theology . . . rooted in a British context,' another clergyman argued. One respondent criticized the church's traditional role as a 'respectable' reconciler, suggesting that the church should take sides, 'having committed itself to reflection within praxis.' Clergy wanted to see that the 'Option for the Poor' Report really meant something, one writing, 'telling the Good News to the poor could (only) be justified because it addressed the social as well as the personal need for salvation'. One respondent felt that the disestablishment of the Church of England was desirable because such a move would identify the church more closely with the poor and oppressed.

The stories of the clergy seem to resonate with the Biblical themes of suffering and oppression which we find throughout the history of the people of Israel from Exodus on. 'The sons of Israel are oppressed' says God in Jeremiah (50.33). Indeed we see it was one oppressive power after another dominating Israel from the Egyptians to the Romans. Even amongst the Israelites themselves, the rich and powerful can be seen to oppress the poor. In Nehemiah we read, 'But see, we are slaves . . . .. (the) abundant harvest goes to the kings you have placed over us. They rule over our bodies and our cattle as they please. We are in great distress.' (9.36-37). In the New Testament the Jews were subject to Roman domination, but there was also oppression of the people by Herod, and the religious leaders. Jesus' criticism of the Pharisees includes the withering condemnation, 'They tie up heavy loads and put them on men's shoulders, but they themselves are not willing to lift a finger to move them.' (Matthew 23.4). Jesus himself was however the suffering servant who identifies with the suffering and oppressed, and 'he took up our infirmities and carried our sorrows. (Isaiah 53.4). He still does.

What seems to be called for is a radical identification with the poor and oppressed. I have often heard it said that what is called for is a radical committment to the areas where riots occur. Some Christians see the black churches with their own particular experience of oppression, expressed in the writing of such people as James Cone, as providing useful insight. In my own experience as a Probation Officer I too found people's experiences of poverty and oppression to be two of the most sinister social evils crushing and spoiling people's lives time and again. It presented a consistent radical challenge to my own faith.

## (2) Taking the side of Justice:

One clergyman asked me, 'Is criticizing police tactics and policy being against law and order?' He clearly felt somewhat disloyal, (whether to church or State I know not), but the important point is this, justice is not

---

[1] *The Kairos Document* (Eerdmans 2nd edition 1986).

simply determined by those 'above' but comes also from 'below'. True justice means listening to those 'below' as well as those 'above'.

Other respondents saw the justice issue as taking a stand against racism. Another, as concerning 'justice and the Kingdom', i.e. bringing the teaching and standards of 'the Kingdom of God' about. Yet another believed 'to proclaim the Kingdom' to be important. Part of this proclamation involved speaking out 'to denounce the amassing of wealth by a minority to the detriment of other sections of society', and to 'bring justice to those who are sinned against by the wider society.' As with poverty and oppression, so with justice, none of these issues are simply matters of personal and individual sin , but also concern the deficiencies of the very structures of society itself. The prophet Micah sums this up well when he asks, 'What does the Lord require of you? To act justly and to love mercy and to walk humbly with your God' (6.6). Christians are to take the side of justice, and in times of riot, as at other times, the voice of justice comes to us from below as well as from above.

### (3) Providing a message of peace, reconciliation and forgiveness:

The Kairos document states, 'The peace that the world offers us is a unity that compromises the truth, covers over injustice and oppression and is totally motivated by selfishness. .... There can be no real peace without justice and repentance.'[1] Christians are called to work for genuine peace and true reconciliation. True reconciliation involves working to do away with evil, not as so often is the case working to accommodate and compromise with it. One of the first steps the Aston and Handsworth Forum of Churches took after the 1985 riot was to adopt a confessional stance, to acknowledge its own failings, and to seek God's forgiveness. This too was an attitude reflected in the replies I received from clergy in riot areas.

### (4) Reflecting the essential goodness of creation:

The clergy survey drew attention to the need to hold a theology of creation which reflected the dignity, wholeness, and equality of all human beings before God. This is the original pre-fall creation pattern, and the pattern of life Christ's redemption brings to those who turn to him. Paul writes to the Galatians, 'You are all sons of God through faith in Christ Jesus. There is neither Jew nor Greek, slave nor free, male nor female, for you are all one in Christ Jesus' (3.26-27). God loves everyone and this is seen in both his acts of creation and redemption. It is his will to set free and loose all those who either through their own fault or the oppression of others cannot enjoy the good life God intends for them. In this respect the particular contemporary issues of racism and sexism should not escape the Christian's critical gaze.

### (5) Proclaiming the Gospel:

Christians have the responsibility to denounce sin and announce the Good News of salvation in Jesus Christ. However, clergy in riot areas pointed out the importance of proclaiming this gospel in a way that shows its relevance. The gospel has to be proclaimed so that it can be easily heard

---

[1] *The Kairos Document ibid.* p.11.

and understood. In history, religious revival has often been accompanied by much-needed social reform. The gospel addresses both the personal and the societal need for redemption.

## (6) Developing a Christian view of the State:
The Christian is called to engage with the process of creating a just and peaceful society. When riots in all their attrocity occur, it is not enough to see these events as having nothing to do with this process. Riots have something to 'say'. The kind of society we hope for has been described, I think very helpfully, in a 1973 World Council of Churches statement. It states

'We believe that for our time the goal of social change is a society in which all the people participate in the fruits and the decision-making processes, in which the centres of power are limited and accountable, in which human rights are truly affirmed for all and which acts responsibly towards the whole human community of mankind, and towards coming generations. Such a society would not be the Kingdom of God, but it might reflect within the conditions of our time that subjection of the powers of this world to the service of justice and love, which reflect God's purposes for man.'

The State will often seek to use Christianity to justify its own purposes. As regards the State, the Christian is always to be in the business of reflective criticism. When this responsibility is abdicated, the State may be able to continue to bless injustice, canonize the will of the powerful, and reduce the standing of the poor and oppressed with impunity.

## (7) Developing a Christian view of the Church:
When the church is seen by many young black people in riot areas as part of the system which oppresses them, this should lead us to ask questions of the church. Often the church is seen as the prerogative of the middle classes; the establishment; and the authorities; or, simply not seen at all. Where it becomes the mouthpiece of a particular social group it easily fails to 'listen' to all the voices and is unlikely to 'act' appropriately. Biblical faith is relevant to every aspect of the social world and all people, and the church's task is to be the vehicle not only for the redemption of individuals but also for the renewal of God's whole created world (as Romans 8.18ff reminds us).

### Third—Action
Perhaps not suprisingly I found the church in riot areas has responded to recent riots in a variety of different ways. There is no single blueprint, and the task the church faces is certainly a large one. One Tottenham vicar wrote, 'It still seems to me that we have not fully tackled (it).' Another felt that there was so much going on with which his church was involved he could not begin to apprise me. Still another confessed to not doing justice in practice to what he felt was being asked of him.

LeRoy's analysis of the responses made by the local churches in Liverpool 8 to the 1981 riots in that city, identified a range of church responses.[1] These included mediation, peacemaking, communicating, proclaiming,

---

[1] M. LeRoy *Riots in Liverpool 8* (ECUM 1984)

helping, caring, protecting, and listening. He also noted the intense 'frustration' felt by some Christians in not having anything to do. This may suggest that some Christians felt impotent and were ill-prepared to handle the circumstances thrown up by the riot. The feeling of not knowing what to do was reflected in at least one clergy reply to my own survey.

The clergy replies to my survey provide a valuable cross-section of real and constructive responses to riots. Clergy were asked four questions. 'What response can the Church make: Firstly, in the period before a disturbance?' Secondly, 'during the actual disturbance?' itself. Thirdly, 'in the immediate aftermath?', and finally, 'In the longer term?'. Their replies when collated indicate what might be done by the church in riot areas, replies which we will now proceed to explore.

## (1) Involvement in the Community:

Many clergy said how important it was to be at the centre of things in the community before any riots began. Without prior involvement it would be unlikely that the church would have any credibility upon which to stand. The church I was told was to be an active participant in the community, not just a respondent to later events. Getting involved with the community might necessarily mean risking our respectability; feeling pain; and standing with the oppressed and feeling with them their powerlessness. It is no good moralizing from afar, the consistent message was 'be involved'. This might be as a community leader, a social worker, a teacher, a youth leader, a policeman, as an ordained person, a journalist, a politician, a good neighbour, etc. etc. Each is to develop their own act of service if they are to retain any authenticity and credibility with the community if and when riots occur. Caring and campaigning give the church a presence and an influence. God, we need to remember, is never 'absent' from his world, but he is never more 'present' than when his body the church serves the needs of others.

Caring and campaigning takes many different forms. Providing employment opportunites, improving the education prospects, opening up a legal advice centre, campaigning for better housing conditions, tackling racism, empowering women to take responsibilities, training for literacy, seeking economic growth for the area, are but a few examples of what can be done. Clergy replies particularly mentioned the need to give power to powerless members of the community, and suggest working with this 'enabling' and 'empowering' purpose in mind.

When riots occur then the caring and campaigning should continue. New activities arise, such as helping the injured and the victims. Christians should offer shelter and comfort. Many will be frightened. Many have vehicles or property damaged. Others experience considerable personal danger. Some will be caught in the crossfire. Some young people will be 'innocently' caught up in what is going on. They may be with friends in the crowd or have looted goods thrust upon them. (For such young people there surely must be a good case for an amnesty to allow the return of such items without fear of prosecution.) Some clergy saw that it was important for the church to set up a 'first aid post' so that people with problems arising from the riots could be 'heard' and helped.

The needs of ordinary citizens, together with those of policemen, firemen, ambulancemen and those on duty in hospitals, should not be forgotten. Undoubtedly the Christians best able to help are those who have planned and prepared themselves for just such an eventuality well in advance. (Even better if all the local Churches are working together). I have been very impressed with the way the Aston and Handsworth Forum of Churches have organized themselves in this way, and it is well worth looking at prior planning in more detail. One example of preparedness is the way the Aston and Handsworth Churches have a group of Christian lawyers prepared to act at the first indication of trouble. Another group of people are organized for intercessory prayer. No-one need feel they have nothing to do. The team can be contacted through the address given on page 5.

## (2) Prior planning:
A crisis procedure agreed by the local Churches can go a long way toward overcoming the commonly experienced impotence that many clergy reported feeling in the face of an actual riot in their area. A crisis procedure involves mobilizing clergy and laity in anticipation of riot events. Ideally, 'looking ahead' means being prepared 'today', making plans, and setting objectives so that no-one should feel that they are not doing the 'right thing', even if that only means staying indoors by the phone when a riot comes. Everyone should know what he or she is supposed to be doing from running a crisis centre to responding in the aftermath.

## (3) Be on the Streets:
All but one of the clergy saw their role to be on the streets as the riot occurred. They strongly believe their presence is important and influential, even though there is some danger of their presence being misunderstood, and runs contrary to the new police policy to clear the streets of all citizens. The importance of their presence is this. Often when riots occur police from outside are drafted who have little or no knowledge of the community or its people. These policemen are frightened and face much provocation. Often too they are no longer identifiable by any visible number, and, encouraged no doubt by this degree of anonymity, police have been known to exceed the restraint expected of them. Clergy strongly argue for their own independent observer role. Clergy, I think, have an important role in evaluating and reporting the events. Sometimes too it is possible for clergy to to take an active peacemaking role and urge restraint on both sides. Being on the streets is a difficult, dangerous and some might say controversial step to take, but one that I too would endorse.

## (4) Listen and Dialogue:
Clergy frequently said how important it was to listen to people, to hear both sides, and to judge the moods and feelings of the area. It was also important to be talking to people, in fact to all who wanted to. Aim, they said, for open and fair dialogue, and work towards peace and justice. Clergy in particular feel that their role is to act as a spokesperson and mediator, but this is a role others can adopt too. The media need to be provided with the 'truth' of the situation. Clergy reckoned the police from

23

outside areas particularly needed to be told of the good in the community. They warned of the danger of always assuming what the police said or did was right. Listening and dialoguing are essential to help reduce tension and calm things down.

## (5) Non-violence:
A Christian presence in riot situations is to be a non-violent one. The Brixton Council of Churches in its statement after the 1981 riots recognized the social stresses which had made so many people angry to the point of riot, but went on to say, 'We believe that appropriate and creative means must be found for the expression of anger. Riot and disorder, however are not an acceptable means of such expression.'[1] I would endorse this position, but with the proviso that it may exceptionally be necessary for people to defend themselves and their communities when facing oppressive State violence.

## (6) A serving and prophetic Church:
Clergy wrote that they would call all local Christians together to pray if trouble was anticipated. This would build solidarity and unity. Beyond prayer, lies a whole field of service. The ongoing work of the church should continue of course, but riots lead to new activity both within and beyond the walls of the church. The church has a clear prophetic task to speak out against injustice and social evils and to announce the Good News of the saving gospel of Jesus Christ. Clergy told of the need to give comfort to those distressed by events. They also felt they had an educative role, telling the story of the riot to those who are ignorant or confused by events. Reflection and Bible study addressing the themes of the riot were also suggested, and this could lead to Christians taking responsibility, for example, to effect social change by political means.

One step forward might be to develop the local church's ministry to be more appropriate to the urban setting, adopting for example the kind of approach advocated by Ray Bakke.[2] Bakke urges Christians to get into the social 'networks' in city areas. He offers concrete ideas for the equipping of the church to do its task.

All in all the riot events need to be brought into the life and worship of the church family and reflected in prayer and worship. And out of this should come the voice of a confident church with a prophetic incisive word for the times and situation in which the church finds itself.

The church outside the riot area, and the national church need to listen to what their fellow Christians are saying in these areas. (This is often the hardest thing to do, harder even than giving money or setting up a link with an inner city church!) It simply is not good enough to decide from outside the situation what the problems are and what is needed to put things right.

[1] In *Crucible* (B.S.R. July-Sept. 1981) p.129.
[2] R. Bakke *The Urban Christian* (Marc Europe 1987)